Red Death, Purple Dark

poems

Thalia Geiger

Thirty West Publishing

Est. 2015

ISBN-13: 979-8-9987727-2-6
Cover design by Josh Dale
Edited by Kinsey Krachinski
Author photo by Kevin McShane
First Edition: February 2026
Printed in the U.S.A.

For more titles and inquiries, please visit:
www.thirtywestph.com

Praise for RED DEATH, PURPLE DARK

"[D]efine the world as this, *RED DEATH, PURPLE DARK* commands: always at a tremor. In Geiger's debut, excavation of our eternally shaking ground, she unearths the divinity in fainting, the simulacrum of flesh, and the appetite of color. Hers is a spell for the starving girls — the stranded and the starry-eyed. A sage for the most hollowed chamber of the heart, to restore what spirit the weight of living has buried.
—AMY JANNOTTI, author of *ANGELS & INSECTS ARE CREATURES WITH WINGS* and editor-in-chief at *Bleating Thing Magazine*

"Thalia Geiger's searing, questioning poems explore the pains and pleasures of "worldly things," of making one's way in a body, in a life, with presence and courage. 'And the trees will bloom just the same,' she writes, 'a hundred-thousand small bombs in white & pink / will be the color of all our deaths.' Imagistic, psychological, *RED DEATH, PURPLE DARK* is a remarkable confrontation to the world's gorgeous fragility—its poems linger in my mind."
—RICHIE HOFMANN, author of *THE BRONZE ARMS*

"At its core, *RED DEATH, PURPLE DARK* crackles and pulses with rotting, devouring, and nature in its many temporal and fragile states. In her debut collection, Thalia Geiger masterfully wrestles with an ever-changing earth, how apocalypses take many shapes and forms, the dualities of desire, hunger, and worldly griefs: "Nothing grows right, not even the / strawberries, whose red death / only bore white fruit that browned / before it ever blushed," she writes in the book's titular poem. "Don't you see everything / lives by dying?" With surprising voltas and a speaker who holds nothing back, *RED DEATH, PURPLE DARK* is both the disturbance and the salve. Like a ripe strawberry swiped across one's mouth in the middle of summer, this collection will most certainly leave an indelible mark on any reader who is lucky enough to pick it up, devour every line."
—ERICA ABBOTT, author of *SELF-PORTRAIT AS A SINKING SHIP* & poetry editor of *Variant Literature*

"Thalia Geiger's lyricism stuns in RED DEATH, PURPLE DARK. Poems woven in dim places & bright ones too, archeology & [de]construction, introspective observation, all extremely important in Geiger's work, but more so poetry is always revelation, Geiger's work too all illumination, evoking rainbows, strawberries, vibrancy & dark altogether, impossible colors bearing witness on the page. Fantastic read."
—NOAH DAVID ROBERTS, author of GUNK & founder of SCRIBES

"Thalia Geiger's RED DEATH, PURPLE DARK, moves like the pages of a modern grimoire, gathering the ingredients of memory and lyrical imagery to make potions of poems that might heal or sear or simply delight. Drink deep in the mirror is the incantation each line seems to sing, reminding anyone, who dares to see, "how thin the line of separation is, from taut to tetherless." Whether confronting literary traditions, personal traumas, disquieting landscapes, or nuanced origins, Geiger's poems anchor their intelligence and craft in a terse truth—we are spells ourselves & should not forget it."
—STEVEN LEYVA, author of THE OPPOSITE OF CRUELTY

"These poems are delicate and raw: poems with the skin off. There is an accomplished level of innovation and technique, particularly in the pair of sushi poems with an initial long poem followed by a stripped-down version of the same poem: brilliant work. There is an admixture of delicacy and power at play here that, at times, smells like Sylvia Plath, in a good way."
—NATASHA DENNERSTEIN, author of APPS POETICA

Table of Contents

Table of Contents

Red Death, Purple Dark

CONCERNING THE END OF THE WORLD

For starters, I'm no Eve L. Ewing or e.e. cummings.
I'm a witch, but I have no powers. I am no
      jewel-adorned fortune teller. I don't know what it means
when a man falls from the sky or a hole
      opens up in the ground and swallows
my cat. I won't know if we're doomed then,
      or if it's the start of a saving. A time for saging
the skies and every crevice we can find with milky smoke
      until we know why the world is
the way it proves to be. Why the bees
      have ceased their stinging. Why we are
butchered—one shot, another paused,
      hard lump at the throat discovered
beneath frozen thumb. I won't be able to warn us
      of the moment I feel a curiosity
seeping through the scalp like a tingling,
      hear a clicking from a golden bug that translates
a message quick and sure as a jostling
      by the shoulders from a nightmare.
When the world ends, I'll likely be sleeping, or else slumped
      over my laptop, sunbathed by the sunset's hues
and clicking some message they won't translate
      until after the man has already fallen,
the ground slick with blood,
      your cat nowhere to be found.

NOTHING'S GONNA HURT YOU, BABY

I was born wanting. Things soft like sweets
that melt in the mouth, dolls in princess
dresses, the material things of a wonderful life.
Button-nosed like my father and a head full of curlicues,
not a vernix-coated baby hair was out of place.
Eyes brown, skin black, sex female.

We made do in our home, cooking like the church
kitchen my mother was raised in.
We said grace and laid old pets to rest
like anyone else. Growing up, the self was harmed,
as selves become. And it harmed, as selves do.
For a while things go right, humming along

and then as if letting go of a final held breath,
they just break. I smiled just as wide anyway.
Wore longer sleeves. Painted my face to look
at something prettier, something I had made.
Some days I chose blue eyelids.
Some days I kept them brown.

My hair sizzled under the flat iron.
I learned to love the sound. I burnt my value
to ash and bred it into vanity. I beat my desire
with a bat and threatened it not to come back
home but I'm sure it had hidden itself in the shed.

I walked a blind man to the subway station
and thought, *This is why you don't help everyone*
when he thanked me by squeezing my ass.
There are often two kinds of pain, one held gently
inside the other like a nesting doll. See how well it fits,
like *laughter* inside *slaughter.* How the surprise inside
is not one at all but more of a disappointment.

MAN TAKING MY BLOOD PRESSURE

He asked what I thought

was the probable cause of my fainting.

I wanted to know what he'd think

of this weak thing he can fix

though I blamed it on the fog

machines at the concert, how I

had breathed in all that fake air.

It is not like me to swoon for nothing,

but it is like me to fall for the man

taking my blood pressure.

I had to ask, do you think fainting

is about the soul not wanting anymore

to be in this body? Trying to ghost

me before I could do anything

to stop it? He laughed, thinking

I was joking, and implied that though

my pressure was low, it was nothing

out of the ordinary, insisting that

it wasn't serious or in any way divine.

I should just hydrate and do yoga.

Worry about more worldly things.

IN A SUBPAR SUSHI RESTAURANT

Settle on something real. The sashimi's a little brown in certain places. If you look long enough, the water glasses aren't clean. Gray finger-smudges color the shaft, someone else's lip print at the edge. The waiter comes, smeared lipstick on a forced smile. Say nothing but, "Thank you." The tip goes. The plate of overripe orange slices stay, bent hides dimpled with oily zest. You leave a tower of naked rinds behind from tearing carpel from pith. Eating is grounding. An act of focus on the feeling, not the light that bounces off of dry hands, illuminating scarred skin. The table wobbles how all cheap restaurant tables do from here to New York, and every other town you've ever been in. You've learned to define the world as this: always at a tremor. It doesn't help.

SUBPAR SUSHI 2

settle on anything you see
brown sashimi
gray glasses
smudged lipstick
you don't mean to say
thank you
the orange slices
are torn apart
eating isn't grounding
what is an act of focus
a tremor
the world never stops
redefining itself

ON THE BOWERBIRD

I am in debt to Maggie Nelson
for teaching me about satin bowerbirds,
the blue birds that collect blue things
to mate. Nests like museums,
each artifact is carefully placed to stimulate
the female enough for the couple to have sex
for two to three seconds, after which
they will never meet again.
In the wild, this is true love: how
a bird, how a human can love
such a thing, a color. I try
to love like that. I am not a princess
of blue, but try to be. Blue nails, navy
sweater, I eat nothing but the moons
from Lucky Charms for three days
to see what she sees. But the sugar,
each quick chomp, chew and swallow
doesn't make me feel what she feels.
It's a crime I've never heard Joni Mitchell's
Blue, so I never tell people.
That's like going your whole life without
ever hearing some white guy with a guitar
wailing Wonderwall. I'd rather listen to
Blue Christmas in February, sit in my azure
socks and bra against my walls reflecting
fishbowl blue for hours until I feel
my insides coloring, each organ and muscle
flushing indigo right before
I realize just how much red
I lack in my life.

ONE NOTE TO SELF

The calendar can't hang itself

until you've marked all the days

of the year with an X.

Your picture is on the wall,

a sheen of adolescence

glossed over vintage film.

The big smile shows off

the high canine, the tooth

whose feet could never

touch the ground.

All these days to make

and be made.

You envision flour,

the mountain that comes

from tapping the sifter

with a flat hand the way TV

taught you, how the little

clump of white accumulates.

You didn't have one

of those until you were

twenty-two, a move-in gift

from a friend's mother

who thought more of you.

You don't even practice
recipes from the Rachael Ray
cookbook you needlessly have.
You make one note to self:
this year, you could at least
take up baking.
The calendar in hand
could become cookies,
blondies, flaky croissants
that display layers
the butter left in the dough.
But don't even think about
stepping foot in the kitchen
until you can stand in there
and bake a cake the right way,
facing the oven's open jaw;
can pull the tray forward
and drag out that golden
lemony mound you've made
without at all leaning
forward to plunge
your tiny head inside.

BRIEF MOMENT IN WHICH I ENVISION OUR BREAKUP

a scene—
brows knitted
a dark brown fresh line
of stitch and slip
across the forehead.
breath ragged and watched
too closely by the other.
this is when the breath
syncs and skips
into a rhythm like
the turning of a wrist
a needle weaving in
and out of the thick.
one bites their lip.
fixates on wood
lines on the table
follows a crack
divot or split
eyes blinking
a dry sting like closing
over marbles for full
minutes thinking
of other things
that need attention:
the trash in the kitchen
putrefying despite
the plastic
sauces stinking
on a plate in the sink
until the other
finally gets up
bored or fed
up and leaves.

MARCH AGAIN

march again and I am drying

strawberry leaves on paper

towels like the witch I am

planning this year to grow again

in the hopes that my thumb

is greener I watch my seedlings

from the windows stretch

their stalky necks heavenward

I am creating a bounty

to sustain us my father isn't sick

and life for once is beautiful

again for as long as I say so

POEM IN WHICH I CRAVE PEACHES AFTER OUR BREAKUP

every season, I like smelling
like something you can eat.
spring is no different,
even with the world ending
just outside our very doors, windows.
give me a perfectly ripe white peach
and I will learn not to crush it
with my hands but sit as a weighted
thing in my palm that only anchors
me back to the reality of dirt.
because if we cannot say no to ourselves
we are the monsters we write about.
because it's impossible to cover oneself
in the creamy white without dimpling
it to a sallowed yellow.
there is no poem that will make
such an abuse make sense.
for every giving bit of skin
that's dripping flesh, there's always
a strong thumb sliding
its way through it.

EXERCISE IN FUTILITY

Already the equinox, and there's ivy
lacing the trees in its blue-green

like it always does. Here in this field,
with the sun warming the earth

in seconds, I feel my futility.
I do try to get out more.

I sit outside cupping tea
and finger the grass like I'm tuning

a piano. I burn pine to ash
and hope it connects me further

to the world. It's the twentieth
time I've tried getting at

the truth, to arrive instead
with a novel of nonsense.

To get to the heart,
I'll have to eat the flesh.

It is true that I am young.
So maybe it is true

that I am not yet
hungry enough.

AMTRAK AS A RED WHEELBARROW

The average blink lasts one-tenth of a second, as fast as we lapse past each tunnel light. In the train car we're in, zipping through New Jersey, I'm reading William Carlos Williams and falling in love with some boy's eyes like molé sitting beside me, the same savory-sweetness you could dip your finger in. "So much depends / upon..." Finish the poem: A rattling pull-down food tray. A Jansport bag on the floor, ever-so-slightly sliding. A glance, the smiling squint eyes make, sleep still in them. I'm not allowed to say more on this. We blink about 15-20 times per minute; more when we're talking to someone, even less when we read, and mine almost glaze over as I do, dryness growing like some furry creature has taken up residence on my cornea. For once, I'm not thinking of where we're headed. Only eyes: how in space, an astronaut can't cry. Tears build in balls and sting the eyes; they never fall. How at birth, babies see only in black, white, and gray; color comes later. How my own eyes, when rubbed, black out and create fireworks of color, itchiness fading to numb fluorescence. And you, now eyeing my book when I'm not looking, about to ask as soon as I blink them open, if I'd ever read *Paterson*.

Too Many Overdoses

It was like that night I saw a man fall asleep
in the street. He stopped amongst the traffic.
Headlights flooded his slackened face,
his clothes billowing loose on his frame
as he slumped into himself.

His curved figure was a question they dodged
with honks, the screech of spinning tires.
Each sound was not enough to wake him
from whatever bliss he was dreaming,
this stranded animal, this starry-eyed child.

RED STELE

they call it red stele a rot
when strawberry leaves

redden almost to purple
and blushing stems

bow drying heads
to the dirt

as a black girl
I also have a black thumb

nothing lasts a full season
besides the weeds

I foster babies
with hydra-like hands

stout stems growing
large and leafy

creatures that cannot be killed
even by their own mother

I am a terrible mother
to kill what I've cultivated

buying reflections of her children
from the supermarket

plastic cartons of others
to stow away

to pretend they're my own
to pretend I can grow

can change my ways
with the moon phases

I'll turn my back
for the scissors
to prune this rot

snip leaves like trimming
a baby's nails.

FORGET-ME-NOTS

I paint flowers by my eyes, small,
pronged and yellow, so every time I see
myself reflected in mirrors I see growth.
But this year, my forget-me-nots grew
mold and I think, this is why I don't
have any friends. A lack of nurturing
surely, a lack of snipping at the sun-fried
ends at the right times. I grab each
ruined pot, dump the dried clots
of soil into the trash, plan to dig
into fresh dirt tomorrow.

TRANSIENCE

only wine-sloshed
do I ever understand
the thought of transience
of a fallen eyelash caught
along the curved cheek
we can't really make wishes
on fallen hairs and dead debris
I have to remind myself
this is only one of the things
wrong with me
obsession over nothing
I pour over myself
the constant grazing
of the skin by my nails
I shred off a full coat
of old polish
that when removed falls
like a petal to the floor
I even pour over
what's in front of me
how here I touch his collar
the ridges of his chapped
lips bright and burning
and yet how
do I look it in the face
how do I meet eyes
all wideness and wet clarity
blinking back open
yielding stark white
and hard core
as if boiled
and waiting bravely
to be devoured?

CLAWS

sharp nails square and thin
on fatty baby skin

need trimming soon

how strange a soft thing can shift
to stiff

to clawing

how quick we watch it grow,
harden

What Do You Call a Girl with Red Hair

queen   spitfire sweet dream
cinnamon fuck buddy
summer lover   sometimes
she calls me   on a mission
to ruin my life   anything but
mine   someone I'd like to pet
can't fuck over   autumn
everything   cherry   copper
-colored   fire flicker   floozy
faulted   gilded   glowing human
red stele like rot on strawberry
stems   bloody ginger
hot tamale like the candies
witch bitch   better than a blonde
anything you want   slippery
snake she is   someone once
said "you love her because
you can't pin her down"
and I thought   *yes*

THIS IS IT, THE APOCALYPSE

The rain keeps coming, murky and hot,
and this is it: the thick mists of the apocalypse,

covering half the buildings downtown
and stretching all the way through the northwest

the closer you get to home. Trees are split,
traffic lights keel over in grief or distress,

creating forks in all the roads.
Power's out in people's houses.

Something is hunting the humans,
finally. Out on the porch, someone is holding

an electric drill that looks like a handgun.
It's something about this area,

all these trees and big streets,
that make me forget I'm a woman

living in a city. No walk tonight. There are guns
out, somewhere. In this kind of heat,

everything dies quick and completely:
like that video of a fox rotting, exploding

into a pile of maggot-filled fuzz. Garter snakes
on sidewalks become sun-dried.

Of course I tried to save one, like I do everything.
Futile. Might as well take the time to find

better places to hide.

BETWEEN ROOMS

So this is all it is,
a bowl of plums tableside
on standby, fake freesias submerged
in cooled resin to liven up
a drafty room. The patio pool
humming itself clean at dawn,
drinking smoothies in the morning
as a way to wait for wine in the afternoon.
Here the air smells of sunscreen,
of transience. A warming
barbecue grill on the fringes.
Insects float deathward towards vents,
their iridescent backs shimmering
black-maroon-green, wet wings
too heavy to do anything but scuttle
or wilt. Eventually everything capsizes:
boats—age-old eggs—desire.
Other kinds of vessels,
sometimes tables, chairs,
a wine glass, a flared temper.
Slivers of the self crack
off. What else are we but heaps
of driftwood skimming the surface?
He and I have been sitting
here for hours out on the patio
half inside, half outside,
as if between rooms.

The house's screen door is open
enough for one of us to get
up and slide through if we wanted,
ignoring the flies, the ants
that crawl over the threshold
and onto polished hardwood.
We accept these critters,
have homes for them in the traps
we have set all over the house.
In the chair he lies in, he turns
his head, wipes off his neck.
There's a bead of sweat dripping
down his forehead he hasn't yet felt
until it trails over his hard brow,
wavers, skips onto the rounded slope
of his cheek. Baked, damp
and drained, we wait for the pool
to clear, for the bugs,
like us, to get trapped
in or sucked under.

INTERSTELLAR

I.

Naked bodies don't rupture in space
but the skin stretches to contain
what's inside. This kind of death
features blasted lungs, bloat, UV burn,
nitrogen collecting in bubbles
beneath the surface, heat and the soul
leaking away from the body.

Mine betrays me this way, in all ways:
the blasted lungs, the bloat. And still skin,
the largest organ, swallows it all.

II.

To look at us through the reflective bulb
of an astronaut's helmet.
How big our heads must look,
how slender our bodies.

III.

Every part of me is dripping.
I tell you to cup your hands
so as to catch me,
so as not to make a mess.
But you just dip your hands into my pooling,
meaning to plug the drip
but all you do is splash,
stain the sky of your shirt a dark blue.

IV.

If we lived on Jupiter, gravity would be 2.5 times more
than Earth's. Like that game we'd play as kids,
readily dead-weighting our bodies,
we'd drop ourselves to the floor,
see who was fastest. Whose body could fly
through space in record time
as if transporting from here to there?
A parent's nightmare, glancing over to the windows,
as summer air blew in through black screens,
seeing their children's shadows drop
in the heat, knees bruised,
my pink floral skirt fanned around me.

V.

Pretend we're not in an aircraft,
black hole-bound and on-course to detonate.
Pretend our hands don't feel this way
with this buzzing.
Pretend we love the things we hate
about each other:
your freckles, faint mustache, and temper—
my indecision in everything.
Pretend I don't still fantasize
about sharp things dragging
along the skin beneath my sleeve.
Pretend time isn't wilting us like flowers.
Your back, my aching feet.
Us dancing around like ginkgo leaves
doing pirouettes in the wind
as if we're readying ourselves to fall again.
As if each turn we make
will somehow shrink us into place.

VI.

W.S. Merwin said it first:
"If I were not human I would not be ashamed of anything."
And here we are, boiling lobsters, trying not
to stare at their button-eyes. Betraying each other
for our wanting—too much, nothing at all—
force ourselves to forget the seismic effects
forever welded to it.

Our footprint could not be larger, or uglier,
the space between the toes too wide,
the arch impossibly curved.

VII.

When we land on Mars,
the red rubble and dust storms
will rub out any marks we've made
when we trudge through the sands.
The dust devils will gouge out our eyes,
warm air rising similar to the summers
we used to know.

NEW YORK AS THE WORLD

Everyone walks so much faster in New York,
you'd swear you'd get left behind.

Every step I take I'm still missing
my train. A man repeatedly hacks

a snot rocket that never makes it
to the ground. I'm so often stepping around

other people's filth that I feel
I've made a game of it, as often life

is filled with games I'm not aware I'm playing
until I realize how often I've lost.

Is there anything else I should be more
aware of? A man puts his hand out for me

to get in the train car first but doesn't move
enough to let me through. I get a fingerless

feeling in my toes. Once I'm on, I'm only safe
until I get off. The sky sinks in minutes.

The vibrant colors become muted.
I think only in abstracts: time, ahead,

looping in on itself into a dark knot.
I blink out the glare in my contact until it all

appears less gray. Until the sky is more open,
starless, and unassuming. I'm afraid

that there are so many men out there
who will make and unmake me.

THE THEFT/ /THE FANTASY

I.

It was our first and only date when he
asked me about my fantasies,
if I had any and what they were,
so we could eventually play into them
one of the next times we met.

I claimed I had none,
having been so inexperienced.
His, he confided, was to dress me up
like a school girl and come after me
with a wooden paddle, suggestively stretched
over a desk while he theatrically tossed his tie
over his shoulder, the whole nine. "Would you
be into that?" he had asked me. I said, *Yeah,*
really meaning, *What the fuck?*

II.

The bird had come and stolen the sandwich out
of my very hands like it was as hungry as I was.
I watched, defensively dissociating as it tore
into my lunch, flying it far to the other side
of the beach, the bread shredded and stuffed
into the sand by its beak. I had hoped, at least,
that I had managed to satisfy him.

Most birds pick up their prey with some sort of grace.
Talons protracted, they scoop up their target like a claw
machine gone right and fly away with their prize.
But I watch shrikes on the Nat Geo channel display
their corpsed prey on pikes in the tree branches,
"like some airborne Vlad the Impaler," the narrator says.
"Anything the bird can get on its spike is fair game.
Lizards, snakes, and even other birds."

III.

After the assault, I yearned to feel sexy again.
I bought the champagne-colored lingerie,
the matching satin robe. I ate strawberries
while I lounged around in it. I wrote this poem
twenty different times.

IV.

I cannot wear burgundy underwear without
him haunting me. My therapist says this will take
some time. We talk instead about what I do
with my hands, where do I hold them when
I'm nervous, and I tell her the usual things:
in my pockets, or out picking my nails
or polish like I'm making depressing confetti.

My therapist tells me to make a list of pros
and cons because I can't make decisions.
I take twenty minutes and two pieces of paper
just to pick out a lipstick. What I want
for dinner: two hours, and several open tabs
detailing recipes for creamy cavatappi. Whether
or not I'll have sex with my boyfriend: days,
sometimes months, and a twenty-page list
of what I'll start to do once I'm healed.

V.

In my head the only thing I always imagine is spring.
Cloudless, the blue sky heavy with bright sun
and every crack in the ground is packed with pink
petals fallen from cherry blossoms. It's warm
and I'm naked, and no one is around. Life is so delicate
this way that I can wear such a thin thing as protection.
I give the fallen petals more use as they cover my nipples,
my eyes. I could bite, grind the soft layers between
my teeth to make a pale paste I'd smother over my lips
but I don't. There's no one to give satisfaction.
None to receive. In this fantasy, there is no wanting.
There is no point, but to find relief.

On Zami and Other Things

I am listening to a taping of Audre Lorde,
her voice patient and not unlike my mother's
when she would ask me a question about myself.

She says, "I have died too many deaths
that were not mine" and I want
to take on the part of the mother,
reach out my hand to pat her puffed 'fro
or smooth it with coconut oil like my mother
did mine, saying, *I know, honey. I know.*

RED DEATH, PURPLE DARK

In the garden, the banana peppers
curl like witch fingers,
or human toes in ecstasy.
The blueberry bush stands tall
but fruitless. The cucumbers
bear nothing yet but one
fragile yellow flower. I imagine
my fate lies in the sun-burnt hands
of my patio garden, this harvest barely
enough for a small, starved girl.
Nothing grows right, not even the
strawberries, whose red death
only bore white fruit that browned
before it ever blushed.
But every year, I see ivy growing
outside of busted windows,
strangling the trunks of trees,
everything begging.
Can you see their desperation
in the purple-dark?
Don't you see everything
lives by dying?

What Made You

When you think of anger, think about how your father once spiked a cake against the wall because he could. It was your birthday as well as his. The candles laid wayside on the table, swathed with thick frosting. You kept your hands at your sides, gaze static on the floor's lusterless wood until he fled, and you could look at the mess he'd made. You love him. You don't understand, but one day you will. You peeled the cake in sticky crumbles from the wall and placed it back into its plastic tin. Had to admit it was a little funny, this innocent cake spattered against the wall like a cartoon scene. The cinnamon spice still smelled the same, flat against the chipped paint. White frosting melted in your hands, grew sticky between your fingers. When you are recalling these moments that made you, remember it all: how almost fascinating it was to watch him snap, how quickly it gave like everyone suddenly let go of the rope in a game of tug of war. Think how thin the line of separation is, from taut to tetherless.

A WEED CALLED BABY

I dreamt I had a weed
growing in my garden.
She sprung from me,
brown and soft-bodied
the way I try to maintain myself,
so there was no mistaking
she was mine, but you know,
in weed-form.
These things can happen
when you're not careful,
a consequence of not tending
to your garden properly,
the way your mom swore
she taught you to do:
You can't let just anyone
in your garden.
Who trampled their dirty feet
up in the pansies,
who ruined the begonias?
My boyfriend tried to love her
like his own, but when he'd look
at her leaves, you could see
something in the eyes
lusting for a weedwacker.
I planned to take her away
before she'd flower,
go on the run
with my weed baby,
watch her dandelion-yellow

smile spread across
petal-soft cheeks.
But in my dream,
I never heard that first
sound of sprouting laughter.
When I woke,
I had somehow missed
that budding beauty
of her face.

ANY ACTION YOU SEE ME MAKE THIS
WEEK IS A STRESS TIC

This week, we tire.
Rack up the debts like change collected
in the pockets and lost in the mechanic swirl
and juggle-jiggle of the laundry machine:
This empty mattress, with no friends on it.
This dirty cushion, crumbed with peanut
butter crackers the mice will love.
This arm, numb.
These legs, sore, and these knees,
always crackling, twisting
like splintered wood in a fireplace.
These candles are burning.
The wax curls: a cooling finger
retracts itself, buckles safely inward
and away from the world.

THE OTHER STRAWBERRY POEM

Blushing, as if studded with achenes all over,
I could call you a strawberry and juice would run
along my wrist should I squeeze your hand
beneath this restaurant table. Waiters would watch,

how I'd let you bleed your color all over me.

KALIMBA

My doctor says
I have no choice but to care
for this body so I take all kinds
of pills now, which clink
melodically like a kalimba
in my palm. I swallow them all
and move on, cementing
this rhythm of heartbreak:
I soar, snap, break back down.
Sickness descends and I'm green
for a while. I take a breath,
run a bath. The water turns
my scars pink. The defiant
knobs of my knees
still protrude above the water,
mountainous as they've ever
been, always breakable.
Eventually, the body heals.
Then becomes luxuriously old
and reliant on aid. Yet beneath
the loosening ligaments
of sun-spotted skin on limbs,
won't we remain the kids
we were, feet pounding down
the corridor running around
in zig zag lines just
because we can?

I HOPE THE LAST PERSON LEFT GETS TO SAY THE WORDS, 'OH WELL'

As we might imagine the last pebble of salt
trailing its way out of the restaurant's glass shaker,
life is going to end in this way.
On its lonesome, gyrating its fated path out
and down the chute, all our hard grievances
ground to the last and final salt.

It will also end with us staring wide-eyed
at the sun, the pleasure of ice cold lemonade
in-hand, lubricating sweat soaked fingers, or maybe
it's a double whiskey that's aged in an oak barrel
poured neat into a well-contoured glass,
whatever your vice or preference.

And the trees will bloom just the same,
a hundred-thousand small bombs in white & pink
will be the color of all our deaths, like the colors
of Vermont snow at sunset & the colors
of fluorescent jellyfish deep in the water
at forty-eight hundred feet

& the colors of freshly bitten strawberries
devoured in the summer heat.

IF IT IS, STILL

Autumn begs us to rest and reflect.
We are standing in a fluorescent

Wawa, in a windless airport,
in my parents' warm home.

I lay my head on your shoulder and let
the bone press against the soft hollow

of my cheek, bring me back to earth.
I have always needed to feel a sharpness

to shape everything else around me:
my own softness, the degree

of my desire. The world is warming
in an endless spring. I miss the soft

death of cold, the way it presses its weight
against me. You keep me at a distance

and I watch it widen until I cannot step
so close anymore. I cannot make out our shapes,

what kind of love we exemplify. Not even
if it is still love that holds us, or something else.

CUFFING SEASON

Like fishing a hair out with dirty fingers
that rub the sclera red.
Micro veins branch out
from tear ducts all the same,
a map of a popular city,
somewhere like London.

It's raining more often.
Leggings, wet-soaked,
spread tighter to the leg
like neon eviction notices
tacked to swollen doors.

Like something you've never seen.
Like animals, hunting, but the hind-shimmy
and clawed-pounce are more like snow skips,
near-silent brushes of white powder
flung from the foot.

Despite the incoming mashed potatoes,
the gravy, the buttered biscuits,
bodies keep fit, so fit
the retainer goes back in, makes a home
of a young mouth grown old.

Like cavities come spring,
there's incubation. Like all these,
but actually a gesture of performance,
coats drawn like curtains

puffed with down and bloated
like snowmen, hiding cards
played close to the chest.

HOW TO BREAK UP WITH A FRIEND

First you drink. Lots of whiskey, until you think your throat is colored blood orange or that deep crimson like those cinnamon candies. Your voice will feel split from the swallow, the cough, like the dry ends of your hair. There will be an aching slope of your back when you inevitably heave into the toilet. Your vertebrae will make space for you, will sway to the rhythm you moan and hum. Medicate the headache, but leave alone the vacant stomach. It'll take care of itself and you, will growl when you think you're alone. Try not to think this is sadness. This is healing. Like pricking yourself with a pin and digging around to get out the splinter, or like a scrape, cupping alcohol in its grooves. Glistening. A small sweetness helps if it hurts: hold a piece of candy corn before the mouth. Bless it with a prayer, then eat away the separation of colors: white, then orange, then yellow. Let sit an hour before moving on.

HINDSIGHT

November, and you still can't see
things the way you're supposed to.
Not the way you could
if you had 20/20 vision
without that squint you acquired
in sixth grade. If only
things had stayed as good
as they were then, all bubblegum
wrappers, Fruit by the Foot,
and games at recess.
Now, there are many mights
that will remain meaningless:
toast still blackened despite you
watching it. Someone to say,
I just can't love you the way you are,
or, If only you had loved me
differently. Every day, the sheets ride
down the hips of the bed and every
night, you stretch to smooth them,
right them. Sometimes,
it's just like this.

AND SO

and so again, Dad is in the hospital
and we touch our chins down
to our chests to pray for a miracle.
we stay inside, not shoveling the snow
that's building walls around us,
though this sickness already invaded
our home. and though grief
has not yet shaken our hands, I have
just barely touched it. it is enough.

COPING

New moon tonight means
you have to clean. Wipe crumbs
off the tables, the chairs,
the floor. Discard the Cheerio
lost from months ago, so stale
even the dog didn't eat it.
There are things that just have
to be done, and this is yet
another one. You wash sheets,
the machine rinse-and-dries
out the pale smell of sleep.
Toss in the rust-colored
washcloths, clear out
the metallic bramble of dishes.
You tremble with the china,
smash a glass: that favorite
mug you'd often cling to
till it goes cold, holding on
to its last gasps of warmth.
You can do this: moving on.
Make yourself a note
to buy a replacement later.
Imagine at the store,
the cute clerk who rang
it up last week will remember
this same purchase, can label
your life with this mug.
He will offer instead a plastic cup.
You are not that kind of fragile,
you think, but you are
moving onto the cluttered cupboard
to reorganize every herb:
cayenne next to cinnamon,
next to cumin. If everything's
in its place, then what
could go wrong?

JUDGMENT DAY

I wonder about you, if another lump grew back,
and about the word "remission," the transience

that's part of it and you finally text me back and say, No,
you're just busy, so I say Oh. And Okay.

But with the orange skies and the way the world's been,
I have a right to worry don't I? Wasn't Jesus supposed to be here

by now? I look for the bearded fellow we all once believed in,
but outside, across the street from my house I just see a white gleam

flash by with the chime of a Mr. Softee truck. Soon the children
will be here and I'll want to go. If you had asked me how

I've been I would've said I just stick on lots of fake tattoos
because I don't have anyone to touch me.

Now I have two tattoos so I feel like I'm always being touched
and though I don't work I work hard to cleanse everything

so I can be pure and at ease. I throw your sweater in the trashcan
so I don't get gasoline all over my back patio. A little witchcraft,

and I have our eight years of friendship inside a tiny bottle
with that perfume we both liked, salt, nails, lemon juice, the works.

When I shake it vigorously I wonder if you're alerted
to the white noise buzzing in your ear. I wonder if you think it's Him.

Early Frost

when we heard the news of your friend
    our broken-machine selves could do nothing
but wait for that other shoe to drop
    and end his life

we all sat in his apartment
    staring at the diamond-patterned rug
and the slightest sound
    could break us

almost all of us whipped our heads
    to look at the staircase
the shuffle-and-padding of careful feet
    on the steps but it was just

someone coming back from the bathroom
    rejoining the rest of the wake's ghostliness
chips were passed around
    the bowl clinked against someone's nails

early frost clung to window panes
    my skin prickled with each tally
of your tragedies and mine
    it shrunk us down to husks

each of us only capable
    in our shrinking to curl further inward
and I thought how like art
    to outstretch the hand

and just nearly touch
    and how like life to retract the self
and never meet at all

HAPPY HOUR AT PROHIBITION

Seven different ciders, fourteen dollar
chicken sandwich, and still I'm insatiable.
It's not just the introduction of the over-salted
popcorn we ate, nor the agreement
that we come here on Wednesday nights
to the same taproom, staring at the birdnoses
at the bar crunch and growl at the mouth,
creating crumbs like falling snow
or flaking dandruff. It's not just
the ambience, though black and broken,
not the sports broadcast in the background
nor the lack of ambition in the room.
There are baroque lines in the walls
of the washroom I follow with my eye.
There's something that pulls me
towards everything: your empty glass full
only of suds, our vacant plate of fries,
that I still want to devour. How hungry
are we, really, if we always leave
the vessels? A cleaved chicken equals two
breasts, two thighs, two legs, two wings,
but what of the carcass? I find it funny
that we tongue our glasses, then wipe
our chins. Peer into the reflection of the bar
and we see animals: a hundred tiny
yellow moon eyes peeking out of black fur.

A Tomorrow or Something Like It

I've had a hard time today
not sinking into the sadness
that built me

so long I've carried
those black stones in my belly
and fed them fear

I've sucked down
raw garlic clove enclosed
in honey for the sickness

and too carried
my old self around
like a ghostly carcass curled

at my feet I took her
to New York and back
like sand between my toes

and the birds still preen
and chirp in bright puddles
and dirt piles amongst themselves

like there is a tomorrow
and so I figure
that there must be one

or something like it
as I sit in my bed
drunk with feeling

while a hawk circles
above my house

THREE SCENES

I.

Only aquarium workers see the fish shit behind the scenes.
On their thirty-minute lunch breaks, they watch the magic
unfurl. Unwrapping tuna fish sandwiches, they listen
to bulbous cries of a lost shark toy, the joyful screams
of a better one found in the gift shop.
By the tanks, the scuba divers remove their swimfins,
humanism returning with each toe curled,
each webless digits stretched. Deadpan mermaids
discard their tails by the lockers, squeeze saltwater out
of auburn ringlets. Like the kids, they note how the scales
look Barbie doll-esque, the same plastic and paint
as water drips off the sequined fins, trickles
into the floor's drain grate.

In this underwater hole, two million gallons
amplify this kind of quiet, the white walls tinging
the whole world steel blue.

II.

Inside the Lincoln Park Conservatory, everyone navigates
around the foliage. Past the fern room, after hi-fiving
small palms to oversized blades, by Peruvian lilies,
blue tangos and big leaf hydrangeas, a father points out
the Mimosa pudica plant that folds up when touched.
Everyone watches him stick his son's pointer finger across
the wire, both of them leaning over to make contact.
Once touched, the child retracts his hand as the plant retracts
its own like a fly closing its wings. In his jeweled eyes
you can see how he lusts for summer, for all textures
beneath his fingertips to move like life beats slowly
within them.

How the eyes, stark and wide, are making sense
of hidden things, how any action can mean more
than what he sees.

III.

A father navigates his walker for the first time
across the living room as his daughter scans the rug
for potential threats, something to catch under the wheel
and throw him off balance—a rogue sock, the cat's yellow
felt mouse that always trails underfoot, some wire,
a stray pen, another fall. It happened too easily:
the blood that pooled from his split chin like strawberry syrup,
leg compromised in two places. She knows now
how bodies are this fragile, and his left knee barely bends
as he hobbles. This townhouse with all its stairs
and narrow halls. This young heart in a body grown old.
The girl waits and hears the rubber soles drag now
on the hardwood, listening to the thump, the wheeze
of the walker shifting beneath him.

He doesn't fumble. Just makes a simple turn
around the bend of the coffee table,
feet scuffing another lap across the floor.

HOW THE BODY CAN SLEEP AT NIGHT

How the body can sleep at night after a fight is a learned thing. Sync up your breath to the rhythmic clacks of a distant keyboard, and keep the mouth agape to accommodate the stuffy nose. Keep tissues close by for the tears that will come. Your fists, fingers can relax now, can soften down like a foldable chair. There's no need to scratch chasms into yourself. Once you start, there's no way to will oneself to stop a flow, whether of blood, tears, or mucus. Still the body. Feel a pain in the abdomen. This is almost always normal. Relax your fingers on the belly's cove. Exhale the inlet to a leveled land and focus on the phosphorescence of a blinking TV light, a heater, a charging cord. Let the tongue sit thick in your mouth as static as the skin's fixed buzz. White noise should be enough to trick the body to an instant slumber.

WHAT LITTLE I CAN DO

Right now someone's playing a piano in a hotel lobby in Kyiv
waiting for more predicted bombs to rain down and I'm here
at my desk writing, failing. I love myself now and by extension,
hate the world, it's cold nights, celebrity races, celebratory
performance activism. It took a long time to realize I need
to stay here, for whatever reason, for any reason. With this body
widening, the mind shrinking. I am terrified of them. What little
I can do but sit here and trace along the delicate swirls of wood
beneath my fingers, and wait. What little I can do but later light
a candle for the world, and wait.

In Bed

Here, he hovers a hand
above her body:
cliff of knuckle,
slope of wrist bone,
near-hairless forearm
laid across rung of rib.

Says, "I love your skin,"
meaning the texture, its sleekness.
Though the mind can't help
but wander to its tea tint
a few notches darker than honey.

His is marble, borderline-opal
beneath daybreak coming soon
through the windows.
She is not stupid enough
to say that he makes her love
herself more than she does.

She is aware of the contours
she possesses, how her thighs shout
through jeans and chafe, conjure up
fabric pillings like charming snakes
that twist and curl
from reclined spirals.

Like dough, he admires the shape,
the cushion that gives.
She lets him as they lay
in their own heap upon the bed,
pushing tomorrow further
with each stroke made
until he presents her an offering:
two slicked fingers that say, Taste this.
And take into yourself
all of you.

End of a Poem I Have No Beginning To

and now I'm cracking my knuckles again,
swirling milky Thai sauce on the stove.

Upstairs my father hobbles on crutches,
each careful thump counting the seconds for me

one-two, three-four across the hardwood.
A soft gurgle from the pot prompts me

to stir again, reminds me how things require
our attention as a popped bubble splashes the tip

of my nose. I could drink this whole boiling pot.
Burn away the hunger sitting thick in the throat

before something, before everything builds
to a fine point, a shared pitch:

the rice cooker hissing on the counter,
a fledgling ticking its beak against the window.

Down the street, a runaway bride
clicks heels against pavement,

thinking her life is over—

All the sounds in the world at this moment.
All the blisters her cold feet must hold.

ACKNOWLEDGMENTS

An endless thank you to the journals, anthologies, & magazines that published the following poems, giving my early work a lovely home:

"On the Bowerbird" in *Atlanta Review*
"Nothing's Gonna Hurt You, Baby" in *New York Quarterly*
"Between Rooms" in *Aurora*
"Amtrak as a Red Wheelbarrow" in *Santa Ana River Review*
"Cuffing Season" in *Black Horse Review*
"I Hope the Last Person Left Gets to Say the Words 'Oh Well'"
in *Wingless Dreamer*
"Judgement Day" in *Tilde~*

I immensely thank the writers that taught and nourished my writing throughout my fabulous and formative years at UArts: Elise Juska, Zach Savich, Sebastian Agudelo, Steven Kleinman, and Elizabeth Scanlon. This book exists because of their collaborative support, creative input, and valuable advice—of which I'll always be grateful.

A deep and daily thanks to my family for continuously reminding me that I'd never regret pursuing my craft. You were always right. Thank you for always being right.

And to Kevin, my ten-year-strong muse. Here's to more life, and more poems.

ABOUT THE AUTHOR

Author photo by Kevin McShane

Thalia Geiger is a poet and editor. She is the author of the chapbook, WILD LIKE A WOMAN (Finishing Line Press, 2025), and has work featured in *New York Quarterly, Allegory Ridge, Coffin Bell, Grim & Gilded* and more. She hails from Philadelphia, where she works in journal publishing. You can check out her website at thaliageiger.com and find her on Instagram @thalierr

ABOUT THE PUBLISHER

Escape the Mundane | Est. 2015 in Pennsylvania

Follow us on:

Scan the QR code to visit:

www.thirtywestph.com